She's Notorious: Unveiling Overt and Covert Narcissistic traits in Females.

By

Ashley E. Eaton

INTRODUCTION

Untangling the subtleties of female narcissism reveals a sophisticated analysis of both overt and covert qualities, ending in the fascinating persona of the famed woman. In this investigation, we go beyond stereotypes, questioning expectations about narcissistic behavior, which is typically associated with men. "She's Notorious" delves into the subtle forms of narcissistic tendencies in women, bringing light on the interplay between overt grandiosity and covert manipulation.

The trip into the feminine narcissistic mentality is an engrossing narrative that traverses the spectrum from seductive self-assurance to more subtle kinds of manipulation and emotional abuse. As cultural expectations change, so do the ways narcissistic tendencies show in women, necessitating a more sophisticated understanding of power dynamics and social structures. This investigation is not an attempt to demonize, but rather an opportunity to better understand the complex network of behaviors that contribute to the mysterious female narcissist.

"She's Notorious" strives to create a deeper understanding of these multifaceted personalities by recognising both overt and hidden expressions, challenging stereotypes and fostering a more empathic discourse on the subtleties of narcissism in women.

CHAPTER 1

1.1 WHAT IS NARCISSISM?

Havelock Ellis, a British author and physician, was the first to identify narcissism as a psychiatric disease in 1898. Narcissism is defined by an inflated self-image and fantasy addiction, extraordinary coolness and composure disrupted only when the narcissistic confidence is questioned, and a tendency to take people for granted or abuse them.

Narcissus Syndrome is called after the mythological character who fell in love with his own image. Narcissism is a normal part of child development, according to Sigmund Freud, but it is considered a disease after puberty. In

psychology and personality theory, narcissism is one of three unfavorable personality qualities known as the "dark triad"—the other two being Machiavellianism and psychopathy.
Clinical examination is frequently used to identify narcissistic personality disorder.

The fifth edition (2013) of the Diagnostic and Statistical Manual of Mental Disorders (DSM) defines it in terms of grandiosity and attention-seeking personality traits, as well as significant impairments in personality functioning—such as looking excessively to others for self-esteem regulation, viewing oneself as exceptional, having impaired empathy, and having mostly superficial relationships.

These characteristics stay generally steady over time and are not primarily due to a medical condition, drug usage, or the individual's developmental stage. Researchers have also looked into a less extreme version of narcissism known as the narcissistic personality type.

These people exhibit most or all of the symptoms of narcissistic personality disorder yet are deemed to be within the normal range of personality. People with narcissistic personality disorder or the narcissistic personality type are obsessed with maintaining excessively optimistic self-concepts.

They become too obsessed with receiving positive, elevating feedback from others, and they react with intense good or negative emotions when they achieve or fail to gain proof that others consider them highly. Narcissists need favorable feedback about themselves and deliberately manipulate people in order to gain or extort admiration. As a result, narcissism is regarded to be a chronic kind of interpersonal self-esteem control.

Those suffering from narcissistic personality disorder exhibit tremendous energy, talk about future success plans, and speak in inflated language and movements. If others fail to meet their expectations for employment, money, vehicles, or houses, narcissists may believe they are failures.

Narcissists will appear confident, self-assured, and psychologically sound on the outside.Researchers and doctors observe considerable variances in people with this condition, implying that not all narcissists act, think, or feel the same way.

1.2 THE SEVEN TYPES OF NARCISSISM

The only formal diagnosis related to narcissism is the overt narcissism defined in the DSM criteria of NPD. However, many mental health therapists who have worked with NPD patients, as well as personality disorder experts, have recognised five different narcissistic personality disorder kinds.

Overt narcissism, covert narcissism, antagonistic narcissism, communal narcissism, and malignant narcissism are examples.

Some experts distinguish between adaptive and maladaptive narcissism, the sixth and seventh potential forms. People with narcissistic features, on the other hand, do not, by definition, exhibit narcissism that is as maladaptive as someone with NPD. Narcissism significantly damages the lives of someone with NPD and would never be called "adaptive."

Adaptive narcissism can be compared to the standard (and developmentally normal) "me first," "the world revolves around me," centeredness that toddlers and teenagers exhibit as they grow older. However, early indicators of narcissism in children may lead to a later diagnosis of NPD (the illness is not usually diagnosed in adults under the age of 18).

•Overt Narcissism :

The "classic" and most visible type of NPD is overt narcissism.

Someone with overt narcissism is overly concerned with how others perceive them. Because of their grandiosity and sense of entitlement, they are frequently unduly fixated on status, fortune, flattery, and power.

Overt narcissists may be high achievers who are extremely sensitive to criticism, no matter how minor.

•Covert Narcissism :

Covert narcissism is less evident than overt narcissism. It is also known as closet narcissism or vulnerable narcissism.

Someone with covert narcissism, like other people with NPD, has an inflated sense of self-importance and needs admiration from others.

A person suffering from covert narcissism, on the other hand, may exhibit more subtle and passive negative behaviors. Instead than bragging about themselves or demanding respect, they may resort to blaming, humiliating, manipulating, or emotional neglect to achieve their goals and keep the spotlight on themselves. They may also regard themselves as a victim.

•Antagonistic Narcissism :
Competitiveness, arrogance, and rivalry are characteristics of antagonistic narcissism. While persons with narcissistic characteristics may be unduly concerned

with how they appear to others, hostile narcissists are especially obsessed with coming out "on top."

To advance, someone with hostile narcissism may strive to exploit others. In order to obtain the upper hand or appear dominating, they may put people down or create conflicts.

•**Communal Narcissism:** Someone suffering from community narcissism, like someone suffering from covert narcissism, may not appear to be ego-driven at all. They may appear selfless or even martyrish at first. Their internal motivation, however, is to gain praise and admiration rather than to aid others.

To that purpose, people with communal narcissism put themselves at the forefront of social causes or groups, frequently as the movement's leader or face. People with communal narcissism believe they are more empathetic, kind, or unselfish than others and frequently exhibit moral outrage.

•Malignant Narcissism :

Malignant narcissism is frequently perceived as the most severe or potentially abusive form of NPD.

Malignant narcissism is characterized by the same egocentric self-absorption and sense of superiority as other narcissistic behaviors, but it also includes characteristics linked with antisocial personality disorder (ASPD), such as hostility, paranoia, and a lack of empathy. They may even be sadistic in nature.

Adaptive Versus Maladaptive Narcissism

It's critical to understand that not everyone with NPD looks, acts, or behaves the same way.

One individual with NPD, for example, could be a well-dressed, charming overachiever who cultivates a certain image to please others. Another example of NPD is an underachiever who has a sense of entitlement and sets low goals for oneself.

•**Adaptive narcissism** is a term used by some researchers to describe narcissistic features such as a sense of authority and a desire to become self-sufficient.7 These characteristics can genuinely assist a person in achieving success in particular areas of life, such as their work, education, or wealth.

•**Maladaptive narcissism:** on the other hand, refers to narcissistic traits such as being exploitative, condescending, and aggressive because they have a negative impact on the individual who exhibits them and the people with whom they engage.

1.3 OVERVIEW OF OVERT AND COVERT NARCISSISM.

Overt Narcissist

A grandiose, attention-seeking narcissist is consumed with dreams of endless success, power, intelligence, beauty, or ideal love. These narcissists believe they are innately entitled and superior, which often leads to deceptive behavior in order to gain respect and power.

A lack of empathy and self-absorption are typical characteristics of an overt narcissist. Overt narcissism is characterized by exaggerated self-importance and a lack of empathy.

Overt narcissists frequently inflate their accomplishments, demand special treatment, and use others for personal benefit. Others may see them as accomplished, but anxiety and low self-esteem lurk beneath their phony exteriors.

Covert Narcissist

Because they are not outwardly confrontational in their attempts to appear prominent, covert narcissists go under the radar. They may be more sensitive to criticism, struggle to fit in, or use self-deprecating language to get attention. Overt narcissists, on the other hand, are just interested in taking up space. They want to be acknowledged by everyone and can manipulate and exploit people through charm.

A "covert narcissist" is someone who has narcissistic personality disorder (NPD) but does not exhibit the grandiose feeling of self-importance that psychologists associate with the disorder.

Covert narcissism is sometimes known as "closet narcissism" or "introverted narcissism." Researchers prefer the label "vulnerable narcissism," because patients with this subtype of NPD appear to be lacking in self-confidence.

Overt vs. Covert Narcissism

Overt narcissists proudly express typical narcissistic characteristics, but covert narcissists do well to conceal their problematic behaviors, thoughts, and feelings. They will appear ambitious, insulting, and demanding by portraying themselves as unique, significant, and entitled, regardless of the needs and desires of others.

Overt or grandiose narcissists' arrogance and self-importance will be obvious shortly after engaging in conversation with them.Similar thoughts and sentiments will be experienced by the covert narcissist, but they will be less visible in their presentation of individuality. As a result, friends and coworkers may take longer to notice the features.

1.4 WHAT EXACTLY IS OVERT NARCISSISM?

Do you have a problem with someone who appears to have an exaggerated sense of self-importance, continually seeking attention and adoration from others while ignoring their feelings? You could be dealing with a blatant narcissist.

In this post, we will look at the symptoms and causes of overt narcissism, as well as provide examples of overt narcissists and practical advice on how to cope with it. Continue reading to find out more about this persistent and damaging personality trait.

An overt narcissist is characterized by grandiose behavior, a craving for praise, and a lack of empathy for others. They have an exaggerated feeling of self-importance and may assume they are better than others.

They frequently want attention and praise from others and may employ manipulative tactics to achieve their goals. Overt narcissists may also dismiss or dismiss others' feelings and needs, thinking them as lesser to their own.

This behavior is frequently accompanied by a sense of entitlement and a failure to accept responsibility for their acts.

It is critical to recognise the warning signals of an overt narcissist in order to protect oneself from their destructive behavior. Knowing how to cope with an overt narcissist can help people maintain their emotional and mental well-being and prevent additional harm to themselves and others.

It's crucial to remember that, while dealing with an overt narcissist can be difficult, it is feasible with the correct methods and support.

Narcissists are easy to identify. They are extravagant, demand attention, and crave praise. They feel entitled and believe they are better than others. They frequently display their superiority by boasting about their successes, criticizing others, or dominating conversations.

CHAPTER 2

2.1 OVERT NARCISSIST WARNING SIGNS

Recognising the symptoms of an overt narcissist is critical for understanding their behavior and controlling their impact on others. Here are some obvious signs of a narcissist:

1. Excessive self-importance and self-indulgence:

Overt narcissists frequently have an overinflated feeling of self-importance and believe they are superior to others. They have a tendency to overstate their achievements, talents, and abilities.

2.Overt Narcissists' desires Constant desire for recognition and admiration:

Narcissists desire the attention and praise of others and will go to any length to obtain it. To bring attention to themselves, they may dress provocatively, brag about their accomplishments, or engage in other attention-seeking behaviors.

3. Lack of compassion for others:

Overt narcissists struggle to understand and empathize with the emotions and feelings of others. They may discard or disregard other people's feelings as trivial or irrelevant.

4. Confidence in their own superiority over others:

Overt narcissists frequently regard themselves as superior to others, including friends, family, and coworkers. They may look down on or insult others in order to raise their own ego.

5. Abusive behavior towards others:

Narcissists often take advantage of people for their personal gain. They may manipulate or use others to achieve their goals, with no regard for the sentiments or well-being of the other person.

6. **Easily enraged or defensive when challenged or criticized:**

When their behavior is challenged or criticized, overt narcissists may respond with wrath or defensiveness. They may become hostile or dismissive, resorting to slurs or personal assaults.

2.2 THE ROOT CAUSES OF AN OVERT NARCISSISM

There is no single source of overt narcissism; rather, it is likely impacted by a combination of factors such as genetics, environment, and personality development.

Here are a few possible contributors:

1. **Molecular Biology:**

According to certain research, genetics may play a role in the development of narcissistic traits such as overt narcissism. People with a narcissistic family history are more prone to develop these tendencies themselves.

2. **Parental Style:**

The way children are reared can also influence the development of narcissistic characteristics. Children who are regularly praised and rewarded for their accomplishments while being held accountable for their errors may acquire an attitude of entitlement and superiority.

Children who are frequently mistreated or criticized may develop low self-esteem, which can contribute to narcissistic tendencies as a means to compensate for feelings of inadequacy.

3. Childhood Adversity:

Abuse or neglect in childhood can also lead to the development of overt narcissism. In some situations, a child may develop narcissistic characteristics as a way of coping with the trauma and feeling a sense of control and power.

4. Cultural Aspects:

Narcissistic tendencies can also be influenced by societal standards and cultural values. Success and performance are highly prized in some cultures, which can contribute to the development of a sense of entitlement and superiority.

5. Personality Traits:

Certain personality qualities, such as poor agreeableness and strong extraversion, may also help to develop overt narcissism.

In the last blog entry, What is Narcissism, Signs and Causes, I examined the causes of Narcissism.

Examples of overt Narcissists

Here are some examples of obvious narcissism:

•Someone who is always bragging about their accomplishments and seeking praise and attention from others.

•A manager who disparages their employees and takes credit for their efforts while bragging about their own achievements.

•A spouse who constantly demands to be the center of attention and dominates talks.

•A friend who always has to be in charge and takes all decisions without considering the opinions of others.

•A public figure who exaggerates their accomplishments and success while criticizing and demeaning those who do not match their expectations.

•An individual who disregards the sentiments and needs of others in order to achieve their goals through manipulation.

2.3 DEALING WITH AN OVERT NARCISSIST

Dealing with an overt narcissist can be difficult, but here are some strategies to consider:

1. Establish Limits:

Overt narcissists feel entitled and may try to dominate conversations or demand attention. Setting clear boundaries and stating your own demands can help you avoid repeating this behavior.

2. Do not Participate In Their Game:

Overt narcissists frequently engage in one-upmanship and may try to elevate themselves by knocking others down.

Don't play this game, and don't take their remarks personally.

3. **Restrict Your Exposure:**

Limit your contact with obvious narcissists if at all feasible. This could include avoiding social gatherings where they will be present or limiting interaction with them at work.

4. **Don't Stroke Their Ego:**

Overt narcissists live on praise and approval. Giving them too much praise or attention will simply reinforce their bad behavior.

5. Remain Calm and Confident:

Overt narcissists may try to elicit a reaction or gain a reaction from you. In your dealings with them, remain calm and confident, and don't allow them to press your buttons.

6. Seek Assistance:

Having to deal with a blatant narcissist can be unpleasant and draining. Seek the help of friends, family, or a therapist who can listen and help you build coping methods.

Last Thoughts

To summarize, an overt narcissist is someone who exhibits grandiose behavior, a need for adulation, and a lack of empathy for others. They have an overinflated feeling of self-importance and may engage in deceitful behavior to achieve their goals.

Childhood trauma, cultural and socioeconomic influences, and genetic predisposition are all variables that might contribute to overt narcissism. While dealing with an overt narcissist can be difficult, keep in mind that you are not accountable for their actions.

You may protect yourself from the detrimental impacts of an overt narcissist's behavior by setting boundaries, practicing self-care, and seeking professional help if necessary.

It is possible to handle the complexity of a relationship with an overt narcissist while safeguarding your own well-being with understanding, empathy, and tenacity.

Is it possible for an overt narcissist to love?

An overt narcissist may have sentiments that they describe as "love," but their experience of love may differ from what most people perceive love to be.

Overt narcissists are usually more concerned with themselves and their own wants and needs than with the wants and feelings of others. They may be drawn to people who they believe would elevate their status or reflect favorably on them, rather than being really interested in the person.

Overt narcissists may also suffer with intimacy and vulnerability, making it difficult for them to connect emotionally with others. Relationships may be viewed as a means to meet their own needs rather than as a partnership based on mutual respect and support.

While an overt narcissist may pretend to love someone, their affection may be focused on what the other person can do for them rather than real concern for the individual. They may also be quick to cut ties with those who no longer meet their requirements or who threaten their sense of superiority

2.4 COVERT NARCISSISM

What Exactly Is a Covert Narcissist?

Covert narcissists, also known as weak narcissists, are emotionally delicate and sensitive to even minor criticism. They appear concerned and nervous, as well as bashful, cautious, and self-deprecating.They frequently evaluate and judge themselves in terms of happiness, assets, and relationships against what others have.

A covert narcissist exhibits more subtle narcissistic traits such as hypersensitivity to criticism, chronic envy or jealousy, gaslighting, lack of empathy, and beliefs of superiority. In contrast to most narcissists, who can be bombastic and extroverted, covert narcissists are often introverted and better at concealing emotions of self-importance. This can make it simpler to succumb to their harmful behaviors.

COVERT NARCISSISM TRAITS

While numerous covert narcissistic features overlap with overt narcissism, their outer manifestations will be significantly different. In contrast to overt narcissists, covert narcissists appear more emotionally open and vulnerable. The fundamental goal of their behaviors, however, is to satisfy their narcissistic supply, maintain control in their relationships, and meet their own demands.

The following are frequent covert narcissist characteristics:

•**Self-serving empathy:** A covert narcissist may appear to demonstrate empathy, but their ultimate goal is to persuade you to interact with them so they may service their own needs in some way.

•**Inflated feeling of self-importance:** A covert narcissist may utilize subtle clues to assert superiority over others. For example, rather than confronting someone directly, they may roll their eyes throughout a conversation.

•**Excessive need for admiration:** To gain attention, a covert narcissist may utilize a "woe is me" strategy, asking others to pity or reassure them.

•**Appearing timid or withdrawn:** Outwardly presenting as an introvert assists a covert narcissist to disguise and defend their anxieties. When they start talking about themselves, however, there will be an underlying sense of superiority and disdain.

CHAPTER 3

3.1 TEN FEMALE COVERT NARCISSIST CHARACTERISTICS

The more introverted side of NPD is known as covert narcissism (also known as sensitive narcissism). A covert narcissist has the same vulnerabilities as an overt narcissist, but internalizes their sense of self-importance, frequently while hyper-focusing on their need for attention.

While they share comparable characteristics, the difference between overt and covert narcissism is all in how a person presents themselves and expresses those characteristics. "When you are in a room with a Narcissist, the traits are spotted immediately" They are Obnoxious.

They're abrasive. They make a huge deal out of their presentation." "However, covert narcissists are folks who fly under the radar. Even if you've been with someone for years, their covert narcissism may be so subtle that you aren't even aware of it for a long time."

That is what makes covert narcissism more destructive and more difficult to regulate. Take, for example, how we react to rage. Whereas an overt narcissist may display their rage in apparent, forceful ways, a covert narcissist may channel their rage inside by becoming self-deprecating or engaging in passive-aggressive behavior. In certain situations, a covert narcissist may even be better at vengeance since they repress their genuine feelings.

If you don't recognise a covert narcissist has a problem, you may not know how to manage or preserve the relationship with that person — and for the covert narcissist, being conscious of anything unpleasant happening is much more difficult. "Covert Narcissists don't have the ability to feel like what they are doing is wrong " Dr. Albers says. "They often feel like they are misunderstood by other people."

Covert narcissism, like overt narcissism, may have genetic foundations, early trauma, and acquired behavior from parents or other carers.People sometimes have the misconceptions that covert Narcissists are not mean ,just to be mean.

Unfortunately that's not what's happening, "Dr Albers said. They struggle a lot,and it starts from feeling very lonely and bad about themselves. Still,they are trying to meet their demands by doing what they know how to do best "harmful activities"

Female covert narcissists exhibit the following characteristics:

1. Dissatisfaction:

A female hidden narcissist is a negative influence. She is perpetually sad and dissatisfied. She is always looking for someone or something to criticize. She does this because if everything 'out there' is horrible, she must be unique and good. It's their method of making everything look ugly in comparison to themselves.

They are emotional vampires as a result of this tendency. You can't be in their company for long without becoming angry and exhausted. They have a deep shame wound that makes them believe they are imperfect. So they have to transfer this shame onto external items so that your attention isn't focused on their defects but on the flaws 'out there'.

2. Victim Psyche:

She pretends to be a victim in order to dodge accountability, shift blame, and gain sympathy. You can't have a normal conversation with her because she will transform practically any topic into a sob story in which she is the victim.

She also fishes for compliments by making a negative statement about herself.

She loses all rationale and may even turn to lying while doing these things. For example, she may accuse you of failing to assist her in a moment of need despite the fact that you did. She must always portray herself as a victim.

3. **Ineffective Communication:**

She has no idea of limits. She is unable to convey her demands and emotions in a healthy manner. When she is upset, she causes everyone around her to be upset so that they can feel what she is feeling.

Similarly, she can be lousy at listening to you and seeing things from your point of view.

4. **Absence Of Accountability:**

You can't hold her accountable because she never admits her mistakes. She refuses to embrace her flaws because doing so will activate her shame wound. While no one enjoys making mistakes,'making mistakes' denotes 'being defective' in her mind.

5. **Extremely Sensitive To Criticism:**

While no one like criticism, constructive or otherwise, narcissists have an exaggerated negative reaction to it. She rejects your valid criticism or shifts responsibility to you.

6. **Manipulation:** She employs manipulation techniques for two main reasons:

I)To evade accountability and responsibility
ii)To keep power and control

Controlling those around them excites covert narcissists. While power dynamics are a natural part of human nature, she appears to be overly obsessed with power and control. She manipulates others through subtle emotional manipulation techniques.

She competes with your other relationships because she wishes for you to invest solely in her. If you're in a relationship with a secret female narcissist, she'll most likely isolate you.

7. Obsessed With Appearance:

It is natural for people to be concerned about their image and reputation. Narcissists, on the other hand, are obsessed with their own image. Everything revolves around their image. Many narcissists are seen positively by their peers but adversely by their intimate family members.

8. Chilly:

She lacks empathy, believes she is superior, and has trust issues, thus she isn't sincerely interested in anyone. She will appear distant and negligent no matter how hard you try to connect with her emotionally.

Friendships are a waste of time, she argues a lot and She believes these things because she is uninterested in cultivating emotional bonds. She's so consumed by her own negativity that she has no energy left to cultivate relationships.

9. Postponed vengeance:

She is covert because she does not want people to see her narcissistic tendencies. As a result, if you criticize her or say something neutral that she misinterprets as criticism, she will do or say nothing at the moment. But she will remember and seek vengeance later.

10. Difficulties dealing with depression and anxiety: Anxiety and sadness are far more common in covert narcissism than in

overt narcissism, but they may also be far more Because they don't want to be seen by others, Overt Narcissist hide their Depression and anxiety.but the covert Narcissists may be willing to share the information with people because they get sympathy from others. Dr Albers said.

Though it may appear insincere and theatrical if someone becomes too outspoken about their depression and anxiety for these reasons, it does not diminish the importance of their depression or anxiety in comparison to the experiences of others. It doesn't make it any less real or dangerous.

"You really have to be vulnerable to get to a place where you can share that information with other people," Dr. Albers said.It takes a lot of trust or time for them to let out a little bit of what's underneath their outward mask they are wearing.

In instance, one study found that those with high levels of covert narcissism were more likely to repress their emotions often, despite having higher connections with depressed symptoms and anhedonia (inability to feel pleasure).

3.2 CAUSES OF COVERT NARCISSISM

While the causes of covert narcissism are unknown, research suggests that the illness may emerge as a result of a mix of events, includingGenetics is a reliable source.

interactions with carers and relatives in childhood. According to one study, those with covert narcissism may have had more authoritarian parents and may recall incidences of childhood trauma and abuse more frequently than those with grandiose narcissism.

Other studies, however, do not establish the link between childhood abuse or trauma and the development of covert narcissism. More research in this area may be required.

Aggression, poor tolerance to stress, and trouble controlling emotions are also more common in those with narcissistic personality disorder.

Why would a narcissist pick you?

A narcissist will select a simple target. Empaths, easy going people, very sensitive people, and co-dependents are prime candidates. They want to have the attributes of others that they do not have, thus the more positive traits you have, the more valuable you are to them.

Narcissists may be drawn to you if they think you have attributes such as wealth, success, or physical attractiveness. Having a companion who possesses these characteristics will strengthen their fragile ego. The target's self-esteem at the time of initial contact would also be taken into account. They will be an easier target if they have low self-esteem.

If you have recently had a significant life event, such as a funeral, divorce, or a painful scenario, this will also play a role and make you more vulnerable.

3.3 DEALING WITH A FEMALE COVERT NARCISSIST

If your partner exhibits all or most of the following symptoms, she is likely to have a narcissistic personality disorder.Here are some coping strategies:

1. Recognise The Fact:
You must recognise that the woman you are with is a narcissist. She may appear to be lovely and loving at first, but her mood shifts when you make a mistake. You may believe that your flaws cause her harsh and self-righteous behavior, but she is a narcissist, and nothing you do can change that.

2. **Define Distinct Boundaries:**

Create firm and clear limits after you understand how your narcissistic partner behaves. This is to defend yourself from her arrogant behavior while also maintaining your relationship.

3. **Do not let her bother you:**

Her manipulative tactics may push you to work hard in order to stay on her good side. Your efforts, however, may never be enough for her. Instead, believe in yourself and don't allow your self-esteem to erode. Allow her statements to have no lasting impact on you.

4. **Do not criticize her:**

Because of her egotistical personality, she does not take criticism well, therefore try to avoid it as much as possible. Instead, phrase your comments such that it does not appear to be a criticism, but rather a proposal that will help her in some manner.

5. **Speak up when necessary:**

When she oversteps her bounds, you must speak out for yourself. Let her know how her behaviors affect you and that certain behaviors will not be tolerated in a relationship. Do not give her the impression that she can walk all over you without consequence.

6. **Keep in mind that it is not your fault:**

There will be occasions when she will blame you for her sorrow, but keep in mind that you are most likely not to blame. Accept no accusation if you have done nothing wrong. Do not allow her nasty attitude to impact you in any way.

7. **Make Space Between You And Her:**

When you feel her narcissistic tendencies are overwhelming you, establish some distance between you and her. Take a break and devote some time to yourself away from her. Do things that make you joyful and recharge your batteries so that you can heal from any pain.

8. **Refrain From Reacting:**

Avoid reacting to your narcissistic female partner whenever she attempts to gaslight you. Count in your head to six seconds. It is an excellent technique for regaining control when a situation becomes tense. If she doesn't get a reaction from you, she will eventually give up. And you will be unharmed by a gunshot.

9. **Maintaining other relationships:** Do not give room for self isolation from your

family and friends.Being in a challenging relationship might have an effect on your other relationships. Make an effort to stay in touch with folks who are important to you. Having a social group allows you to divert your attention away from stressful situations.

10. **Seek Professional Assistance:**

It is difficult to deal with a narcissistic woman. When you feel you can no longer take it, get help from a competent counselor. You may seek assistance for yourself and, if feasible, your partner. A skilled professional counselor will advise you on how to approach your partner without hurting their or your feelings.

3.4 FIVE DISTINCTIONS BETWEEN NARCISSISM AND HEALTHY SELF-ESTEEM

1. Demonstration:

Overt narcissists are more grandiose and attention-seeking, whereas covert narcissists are more introverted and withdrawn.

Overt narcissists may flaunt their accomplishments and seek adulation, whereas covert narcissists may minimize their achievements and seek affirmation in more subtle ways.

2. Confidence in Oneself:

Overt narcissists have high self-esteem and an overestimation of their own abilities and significance, but covert narcissists may have lower self-esteem and a more fragile sense of self-worth.

Overt narcissists may believe they are entitled to special treatment and recognition, but covert narcissists may constantly seek validation and reinforcement.

3. **Personal Relationships**:

Overt narcissists may engage in grandiose and exploitative behaviors in relationships, whilst covert narcissists may be more manipulative and dominating.

Overt narcissists may engage in affairs or serial relationships, whilst covert narcissists may engage in emotional manipulation or gaslighting.

4. **Expression of Emotion**:

Overt narcissists may express their emotions more openly and powerfully, whereas covert narcissists may hide their feelings or project a fake character to others.

Overt narcissists may express themselves in a grandiose or flashy manner, whereas covert narcissists may be more reserved or private.

5. **Therapy:**

Overt and covert narcissists may react differently to treatment. Overt narcissists may be more resistant to treatment and less likely to seek help, whereas covert narcissists may be more open to therapy but suffer with trust and vulnerability difficulties.

Treatment approaches may need to be adjusted to each type of narcissist's unique demands and challenges.

CHAPTER 4

4.1 UNDERSTANDING NARCISSISTIC BEHAVIOR IN FEMALE GENDER

We commonly consider narcissism as a specific collection of qualities; nevertheless, narcissist women frequently exhibit distinct traits and behaviors than male narcissists. Men, in fact, are frequently labeled as narcissists.

Female narcissism, on the other hand, appears to be more likely to go unnoticed.Approximately 75% of narcissists are guys, according to studies. This could, however, be due to gender biases in diagnosis.Borderline or histrionic personality disorders are more commonly diagnosed in women.

As more is learned about narcissistic abuse, more is learned about these ignored narcissist women.In some ways, narcissistic women may be more harmful than their male counterparts.

Narcissist women frequently utilize misconceptions about women to conceal their narcissistic behavior. They may disguise themselves as a "nurturing mother," a "doting grandmother," or a "helpless and naive young woman."

Narcissists are excellent performers, and they use these personas to divert attention away from their malicious behavior or other ways a narcissistic woman feels.Nobody suspects a woman who presents herself as a caring mother of abusing or neglecting her children. Underneath these masks, narcissistic women are quite violent, and they frequently express their hostility in ways that narcissistic males do not.

4.2 TWELVE CHARACTERISTICS OF NARCISSISTIC WOMEN AND HOW TO DEAL WITH THEM.

Because their phony confidence hides their fragile ego, narcissistic women lack sympathy and the ability to empathize with others. A narcissistic personality disorder is a condition in which a person believes they are excessively important and superior to others.

It's because they live in a bubble of superiority and can't bear even the mildest criticism. Dealing with such ladies might have a negative impact on your mental health.

A Narcissistic lady can have a negative impact on your self-esteem and confidence. Here are some symptoms that you're dating a narcissistic woman.

1. **She is adamantly opposed to interpersonal limits:**

In any relationship, a narcissistic woman does not respect limits. She is self-centered and narcissistic, thus she believes she is entitled to preferential treatment over others, disregarding your need for personal space. She enjoys putting you in awkward situations by frequently crossing the queue.

2. She enjoys your suffering:
She has low self-esteem and tries to put people down to feel better. She makes nasty remarks and overly critical comments in order to make you feel inadequate. Even when you share your triumphs with her, she is snobbish and arrogant, dismissing your efforts as unimportant.

3. She tries to destabilize your other relationships:
A female narcissist would do whatever to keep you under her control, including causing a schism between you and your loved ones. She accomplishes this by spreading rumors about you or producing confusion and misinterpretation between you and others.

James Adams, a narcissistic abuse survivor, writes about his encounter with a narcissistic female colleague who, he claims, strove to outdo him in every setting. "Once upon a time, I was having a very serious conversation with our boss (this was, of course, before the narcissist became my supervisor)."

She entered the room, sat on the edge of our boss's desk, and announced, 'I had a dream about you last night.' He was not only competing with me, but also with the more important personnel in the organization- our boss.

4. She just speaks about herself:

A narcissistic woman enjoys talking highly about herself. She is so self-absorbed, conceited, and obsessed with herself that she exaggerates her accomplishments and creates a great but false image of herself. She will persuade you that she is a beautiful woman and that you should admire her.

5. She Employs The Victim Role:

A narcissistic woman's troubles and sorrow are greater than anyone else's. She may not brag about her struggles in life, but if you try to relate yours, she will turn the conversation to her own and portray herself as a martyr.

6. She holds you accountable for her faults:

A narcissistic woman believes she never makes mistakes, so when something goes wrong, it must be the fault of someone else. She will never confess her error and will always hunt for ways to blame someone else.

7. **She is unable to bear slights:**

If a narcissistic lady catches you criticizing her or speaking negatively about her, she will immediately defend herself. She overreacts to the point where you feel awful and guilty for doubting her. Narcissists want their partners to idealize them even during sex, regardless of how well they behave in bed

8. **She is unconcerned about your feelings:**

Narcissistic people are distinguished by their lack of empathy. Caring for you is not something they naturally do. Even though you have a fever, she still complains about you getting sick on the day she wants to spend time with you. She uses guilt to force you to do things her way.

9. **She oscillates between idealizing and depreciating**:

A narcissistic lady will love bomb you and make you addicted to her affection and attention in the beginning. She will quickly take the rug out from under your feet if she believes you have become dependent on them. She likes to mess with your emotions by idealizing and depreciating you.

10. **She Is Materialistic:**

Because a narcissistic woman values her outward looks and public image, her love is mainly concerned with material gains. When the benefits run out, so does her affection. She will not become entangled with someone who has nothing to give her.

11. She believes that everyone admires her:

A narcissistic woman finds it difficult to maintain long-term friendships or relationships because she believes everyone is jealous of her. Because she is vain and believes she is superior to others, she refuses to acknowledge others' accomplishments over her own, which frequently harms her relationships.

12. She withholds sex as a kind of punishment:

If a narcissistic woman believes you have failed her down as a mate, she will find ways to punish you. Giving you the silent treatment or withholding sex is her way of making sure you never make her feel insignificant or inferior.

Male narcissists are more prone to emphasize their intellect, power, and money, whereas female narcissists emphasize their body, beauty, and sexuality, according to Sam Vaknin, Ph.D., Professor of Finance and Psychology, Centre for International Advanced and Professional Studies, Lagos, Nigeria

4.3 NINE NARCISSISTIC MANIPULATION TACTICS

A person with a narcissistic personality or qualities typically employs manipulation techniques to influence and manipulate others. Gaslighting, triangulation, love bombing, and other tactics are common instances. If you are experiencing these behaviors in one of your relationships or friendships, there are healthy methods to deal with it, as well as professional treatment choices to assist you in healing.

A person with narcissistic qualities may attempt to manipulate another person in a variety of ways. This manipulation is frequently used to obtain something they desire from a relationship, to make themselves look good, or to satisfy their narcissistic needs. This can include emotional abuse, gaslighting, and a variety of other behaviors. These manipulation techniques might be subtle, or they can be overt and glaring.

The following are eleven frequent narcissistic manipulation techniques:

1. **Deception:**
A person with narcissistic tendencies usually believes that they can do no

wrong. When confronted with errors, they will become defensive and may reject your reality or recall of events. Phrases like "it wasn't that bad," "you must be losing your mind," and "it didn't happen like that" are popular claims used to get you to deny your truth. These are all typical examples of gaslighting behavior.

Initially, a person may talk back and defend themselves against narcissistic gaslighting. Changing someone's view of reality, on the other hand, makes them more likely to drop or move on from an argument over time.

When a narcissistic person feels out of control in a relationship, they typically engage in this type of manipulation. This, in turn, can sometimes develop to narcissistic abuse syndrome, particularly when paired with other forms of narcissistic abuse.

2. **The Love Bombing:**

Consider the beginning of your relationship, when everything seemed like a fairytale. Perhaps your companion showered you with presents and affection, confessed their love for you quickly and early on, or lavished you with attention at all hours of the day and night. This stage of the relationship is known as love bombing, and it occurs when a narcissist manipulates you by using your affection and attention against you.

Due to their proclivity to accept or dismiss love bombing behaviors, people who have experienced previous relationship or familial trauma are especially vulnerable to this manipulation technique. However, love bombing is not limited to romantic relationships, despite its most common manifestation. It can also happen in the business, friendships, and family or social institutions when one person is attempting to attract or influence the attention of the other.

3. Triangulation:

When a person attempts to pull a third person into a quarrel in order to benefit himself, this is known as narcissistic triangulation. This type of manipulation can occur in a relationship or friendship, as well as with narcissistic parents. This is also prevalent in the workplace, when a manager or coworker inserts a third party into a dispute in order to persuade them to take their "side" or to redirect attention away from their own conduct.

4. **Projection:**

When someone is unable to deal with their unpleasant emotions or recognise their harmful behaviors, they may project them onto others. In these circumstances, the victim of their narcissistic projection is frequently accused of performing the same things as the individual.

A narcissist who is projecting, for example, may assume that someone else is angry when, in fact, they are the one who is angry but is uncomfortable with this feeling. This can also be seen in love relationships, such as accusing a partner of infidelity when they are the ones who are unfaithful.

5. **Taking on the Role of the Victim:**

After indulging in damaging or vindictive behavior, a narcissist will frequently play the victim, drawing sympathy and attention to themselves. They may do so by claiming that they were the ones who were harmed or exploited, rather than the true victim. They can be highly convincing due to their persuasive nature, projection, and cognitive distortions, and often have outsiders perplexed as to what the truth is.

6 **Smear Campaign:** A narcissistic smear campaign occurs when a narcissist weaves a web of lies or exaggerations to discredit and alienate someone. This is usually done in front of anybody who will listen, including the victim's friends and relatives. For example, suppose a person splits up with their partner, and their ex begins to spread rumors about them throughout their close-knit social groups.

This individual gradually notices that their supporters are drifting away from them and diminishing contact.

As a result, the victim is frequently left with little support, as their loved ones may believe the lies perpetrated about them. When they try to report the abuse, they are treated as if they are the ones who are generating the problems.

7. Seeking Vengeance:

When someone with NPD feels offended, they frequently desire vengeance. This can take the shape of a smear campaign, but it can also happen in a variety of other ways. A narcissist may attempt retaliation at work if they are denied a promotion or raise, or if they are openly criticized in a meeting. In order to make the other person's job more difficult, the narcissist may purposely turn in projects late or skip finishing critical responsibilities.

8. **Guilt Trip:**

They are guilt tripping you when they try to convince you to do something because you feel awful for them. This type of behavior might be difficult to recognise, especially if you don't know the person well or have never seen it before. A narcissist, on the other hand, will frequently use this strategy to persuade people not to do anything or to cede control over a situation.

9. **Vacuuming:**

Hoovering occurs when a narcissist seeks to "win" back a person. This stage is similar to the love bombing stage in that the narcissist may use similar tactics, such as showering a person with presents and praise.

This time, however, it is to win someone back after a split or fight. In some circumstances, people believe they are losing control of another person and seek to regain control of that individual. Sending irregular SMS or messages, liking a social media post, or sending a person presents at random are all examples of this. As a result, the individual gets drawn back into the previous connection.

10. **They specifically target codependents:**
Because they target codependents, narcissists frequently succeed in manipulating others. "Narcissists generally seek out those with codependency

characteristics," Relationship Expert Tom Gagliano says.

"The narcissist reinforces the codependent's flaws by convincing them that everything is their fault or that they are responsible for resolving any problems in the relationship." The partner fears the narcissist to the extent of losing their sense of self by believing all of the narcissist's distortions.

11. **They make you feel unique:**

These self-centered people also go out of their way to make others feel unique, not because they actually value something about the individual, but in order to manipulate them. "In their personal relationships, narcissists most often gain control over others by playing to a person's (very understandable) desire to feel special and highly valued," Forrest Talley, a Clinical Psychologist, explains.

"For example, a Narcissist may say,It's crystal clear that I have just met you,but to me I can clearly see that you are capable and exceptionally bright" .I got in touch with a small group of folks, many of whom are similar to you... I'd like for you to be a part of that group. Simply provide me with your phone number, and I'll add it to my private black book.' (Does this sound ridiculous? It is, but this is what a narcissist told me years ago... no, not a patient).

4.4   HANDLING   NARCISSISTIC MANIPULATION

Having to deal with narcissistic manipulative tactics can be perplexing and stressful. However, depending on whether these people are love partners, coworkers, relatives, or friends, there are strategies to deal with them.

Here are some strategies for dealing with narcissistic manipulation:

•**Develop Healthy Boundaries:** Setting appropriate boundaries when interacting with a narcissist might be critical to ensuring that you have the fortitude and emotional space to decrease the opportunities for them to influence you.

•**Avoid Excessive Communication:** When possible, avoid interaction with a narcissist. When you do need to communicate with them, such as in circumstances of joint custody or family members who you can't avoid, keep it concise and to the point.

•**Pick Your Battles:** Choose what you want to react to. If they are raising complaints about your employment that endanger your work, you should address this. Ignore them if they criticise your clothing style.

•**Sever Ties When Possible:** If you don't have to have contact with the individual, it's sometimes a good idea to do so for safety reasons, especially after a breakup with a narcissist. This will reduce their ability to manipulate you.

•**Practice Self-compassion:** It is natural to feel frustrated, confused, depressed, and other negative emotions while dealing with a manipulative individual. Self-acceptance is important in learning how to love and support yourself after going through a traumatic situation.

CHAPTER 5

5.1 RECOGNIZING NARCISSISM IN PERSONAL AND PROFESSIONAL SETTINGS

Have you ever worked with someone who was so self-absorbed that they "clawed their way to the top" with little regard for others? While not everyone who appears selfish is a diagnosable narcissist, a small minority is. Narcissistic personality disorder (or NPD) is considered to affect 1 to 5% of the adult population.

Many more, however, exhibit at least some narcissistic characteristics, such as exaggerating successes, seeking attention and praise, and believing they are naturally better than others. Surprisingly, men account for around 75% of those diagnosed with narcissistic personality disorder.

To some extent, self-centered tendencies like ambition and risk-taking can be beneficial in the workplace, which is why many successful people exhibit signs of narcissism from time to time. Narcissism can range from healthy degrees of self-assurance to unhealthy levels of entitlement. Extreme narcissism can impair a person's capacity to perform in social and professional contexts, including the job.

People in positions of authority, such as leaders and CEOs, may appear to be prone to narcissism. True, history and some research indicate that narcissists are excellent at gaining power. However, most leaders are ineffective because they lack compassion and struggle to communicate effectively or sustain connections.

Learn how employers may detect narcissistic behavior in leaders and other employees, as well as solutions for dealing with narcissistic people at work and elsewhere, in this article.

5.2 SIGNS OF A FEMALE NARCISSIST IN PROFESSIONAL SETTINGS

Here are some examples of how a narcissistic boss or another narcissist at work may have climbed to prominence, as well as how they treat their coworkers: believing they are always correct and refusing to listen to feedback or advice from others.

•Taking credit for the efforts of gossiping about colleagues, blackmailing people in front of their teams or bosses to gain favor and spreading rumors are all examples of workplace bullying.

•Refusing to collaborate with colleagues who are perceived to be "below" them or not of high enough status.

•Failure to consider the impact of decisions on colleagues or ignoring subordinates' concerns.

•Refusing to delegate duties or share responsibility.

•Tolerating anyone who questions their power.

•Insisting on being the center of attention or seeking favors from coworkers.

•Always returning the conversation back to themselves.

•Taking pride in one's accomplishments or seeking frequent praise.

•Demanding benefits or allowances that others do not have.

•Using excessive flattery, charm, or other techniques to obtain favor or authority.

Narcissist-Friendly Professions

Narcissists work in a wide range of areas and can be found in a variety of settings, from colleges to government agencies. Having said that, self-absorbed and entitled individuals are sometimes lured to occupations that allow them to feel important, powerful, and adored.

Here are some occupations that may appeal to narcissistic people:

•**Business Executives:** Leadership positions in the business sphere can provide narcissists with opportunity for power, recognition, and financial success.

•**Politicians:** A career in politics can bring prospects for public exposure, power, and influence.

•Careers in the entertainment sector, such as acting, singing, and modeling, can provide prospects for fame, special treatment, and admiration.

•Jobs involving control, authority, and the potential to exercise power over others, such as law enforcement and military roles, may be appealing to narcissists.

•**Medical Personnel:** Doctors and surgeons, for example, may find possibilities for recognition and adoration for their knowledge and expertise.

5.3 THE EFFECTS OF A FEMALE NARCISSISTIC LEADERS AT WORK SPACE

Some data suggests that a large number of leaders have narcissistic tendencies or perhaps a narcissistic personality disorder. It should be noted, however, that not all leaders are narcissistic, and not all narcissists become successful or leaders.

People with narcissistic characteristics may become leaders for the following reasons:

•**They are self-assured:** Because they believe in their value, narcissists are willing to make difficult decisions and take risks.

•**They're charismatic:** At first, they can be quite persuasive and likable, allowing them to rally people behind them and their visions.

•**They are highly motivated and ambitious:** They have a great desire for success and recognition as a result of their grandiosity. Some may even be workaholics because they prioritize things like gaining money and getting promotions over spending time with their loved ones.

•**They have no fear:** Narcissists are not afraid of taking risks and are eager to take risks, even in uncertain situations.

5.4 THE DIFFICULTIES OF WORKING WITH A FEMALE NARCISSIST

Narcissists in the workplace can disrupt business culture, communication, and production.

Here are some instances of the difficulties associated with working with a narcissist

•**Productivity Decline:** Being overly concerned about one's image and earning accolades might lead to inefficiency. Narcissists, for example, can disrupt workflows, cause conflicts, or miss deadlines that they do not consider important.

Working with a narcissistic coworker or supervisor can lead to poor teamwork, resentment, and stress since they make the workplace feel poisonous and demotivating.

•**Employee Turnover:** Narcissists can make employees feel undervalued, underappreciated, or unsupported, leading to their resignation.
Negative consequences for team dynamics: Self-centered people are difficult to collaborate with, share ideas with, and create trust with.

•**Negative impact on employees' emotional and physical health:** Spending time at work with a selfish, angry, or insensitive individual makes it difficult to enjoy one's job. The friction and competition that narcissists cause in the workplace might contribute to concerns like anxiety.

The Other Dark Triad vs Narcissistic Personality Traits

Narcissism is one of the three personality qualities known as "the dark triad," which are frequently associated with undesirable behaviors and results.

The dark triad consists of the following characteristics:

Narcissism is characterized by grandiosity and arrogance, as well as the assumption that one is superior to others.

They aren't always violent or clearly self-centered, as is the case with fragile and covert narcissists (also known as "dark empaths," who exploit people's vulnerability).

Psychopathy is defined as a lack of empathy or remorse, a proclivity for impulsive or reckless behavior, and a contempt for societal norms or regulations. Psychopaths have a surface appeal, a predisposition to mislead or manipulate others, and a lack of sorrow or regret, even when vicious and aggressive.

Individuals with dark triad qualities are more prone to engage in unethical or harmful behavior in both personal and professional situations, as well as in relationships. For example, they are willing to knock people down in order to climb the corporate ladder and will take risks in order to obtain authority.

The primary distinction between the three is that psychopaths are more reckless and impulsive, whereas Machiavellians are more cautious and less attention-seeking, and narcissists are more obsessed with their image.

CHAPTER 6

6.1 COPING STRATEGIES IN DEALING WITH A NARCISSIST IN A PROFESSIONAL SETTINGS

If you are concerned about someone's behavior at work and how it affects you, your coworkers, or your organization, you should seek assistance from management or human resources.

Aside from getting help from coworkers, here are some strategies to deal with working with a narcissist:

•**Inform yourself:** It's easier to work with and avoid problems when you recognise narcissistic behavior and understand how narcissists are aroused. For example, avoid criticizing or embarrassing them in front of others, and instead speak plainly without enraging them. If they have a habit of dominating meetings, consider creating an agenda ahead of time or assigning a facilitator to keep the topic on course.

•**Avoid getting involved in power struggles:** If you disagree, stick to facts rather than emotions or opinions. Take the "high road" and avoid feeling obligated to impress someone who is self-absorbed and inflexible.

•**Establish boundaries:** Set clear expectations and refuse inappropriate demands or behaviors. Speak out for yourself, but do so in a respectful manner.

•**Interactions should be documented:** Keep emails and messages, as well as notes from discussions, so you may refer to them later if necessary. This can protect you if their behavior turns hostile, or if they try to "gaslight" you by claiming you don't remember things well.

•**Take Nothing Personally:** Individuals who are narcissistic may be disrespectful or nasty to others. Remember that this is generally due to their own anxieties, not your worth as a person.

•**Find a new job:** If working with a narcissist in a position of authority is toxic and unhealthy for you, consider looking for a new employment that will bring you less stress.

6.2 IDENTIFYING NARCISSISTIC RELATIONSHIPS .

When both parties or one have narcissistic disposition,a Narcissistic Relationship is born. Mayo Clinic deposited Narcissistic Personality Disorder (NPD) as a state of "a mental disorder that makes people have an inflated sense of their own importance and deep need for admiration"

Those suffering from narcissistic personality disorder believe they are superior to others and show little concern for other people's feelings; nonetheless, below this mask of arrogance hides a weak self-esteem vulnerable to the least criticism." The world we live in is becoming increasingly egotistical. Hard statistics and scientific evidence point in this direction.

The "look at me" mentality that social networks like Facebook frequently foster has users positively enamored with the image they project to the world. Furthermore, we may now be witnessing the detrimental consequences of the self-esteem movement on a broader scale. So, how is this growth in narcissism affecting our personal relationships? For one reason, more narcissism results in increased narcissistic relationships.

Professor Brad Bushman of Ohio State University stated unequivocally, "Narcissists are very bad relationship partners." According to research, your spouse in a narcissistic relationship is more likely to engage in manipulative or game-playing behaviors and is less likely to be committed long-term. A relationship with a narcissist can be difficult to manage.

What Are the Signs of a Narcissistic Relationship?

When I think about narcissism, I'm reminded of the joke about someone who goes on and on about themselves, then stops and says, "But enough about me, how do you feel about me?" If your partner is constantly seeking attention and validation, he or she may be a narcissist.

A narcissist is someone who is easily offended or overreacts to criticism. If they believe they are always correct, that they know more, that they must be the best, and so on, these are also indicators of narcissism. Narcissistic people may appear to care about you only when you meet their wants or serve a purpose for them. A narcissistic relationship can cause a lot of emotional pain.

NPD is thought to affect about 1% of the population. However, because many persons with NPD do not seek therapy, they are never diagnosed. According to studies, men are more prone to be narcissistic. Men account for over 75% of those diagnosed with NPD.

Although practically everyone exhibits some self-centered or narcissistic characteristics, the majority of people do not fit the criteria for a personality disorder. There is, however, a rising segment of the population exhibiting an increasing number of toxic, narcissistic qualities that are negatively impacting their life and the lives of those around them, even if they do not satisfy the clinical diagnosis of NPD. Attaching to someone who exhibits these negative features can generate as much misery as a diagnosable narcissistic relationship.

According to a recent study from Ohio State University, one simple question can identify narcissists as accurately as the 40-item test that has long been used to diagnose NPD. The question is straightforward: rate yourself on a scale of 1-7: "To what extent do you agree with this statement: I am a narcissist. (Note: The word 'narcissist' means egotistical, self-focused and vain.)"

You can also take this free interactive narcissism test. While this study reveals that many narcissists willingly admit to having narcissistic characteristics, it is vital to highlight that the majority of narcissists avoid being diagnosed with NPD. Narcissists, in general, dislike being told they are narcissists. They frequently have a significant negative and volatile reaction. The listed below are common traits of a Narcissistic partner (Note: these features reveals themselves based on individual involved)

•Possession of a sense of entitlement or superiority

•Empathy deficiency

•Controlling or manipulative behavior

•A strong desire for adoration

•Full concentration on meeting self demands while ignoring the needs of others.

•Aggression levels that are higher

•Difficulty accepting feedback on their behavior

What causes someone to become narcissistic?

Narcissistic persons frequently have narcissistic parents who provided them with a façade but no true substance. Their parents want that they be excellent so that they might be the parents of a fantastic person, the best artist, the smartest student, and so on.

Narcissistic persons were frequently neglected because their parents were so preoccupied with themselves that they were unable to attune to their child's emotional needs. The child was only beneficial to these parents when it served a purpose for them. The parents of a child with NPD frequently switched between emotional hunger and apathy in the child.

Narcissists have inflated self-esteem (both self-soothing and self-aggrandizing "voices"), which is part of what my father, Dr. Robert Firestone, calls the "anti-self." They are highly vulnerable since the second component of the anti-self (extremely self-hating and self-demeaning "critical inner voices") is very low self-esteem, the flip side of their self-aggrandized mood.

As a result, even mild criticism can be a narcissistic injury for these people, resulting in an angry outburst and desperate attempts to restore their fragile, inflated self-esteem. A condescending remark will frequently assist them in reestablishing their superior image. Condescending behavior is typical in narcissistic relationships. This behavior stems from narcissists' intense desire to be superior to others.

6.3 CONSEQUENCES OF HAVING NARCISSISTIC PARTNER IN A RELATIONSHIP

Narcissism exists on a scale, and some degree of self-focus can be deemed healthy while maintaining functional relationships. When self-involvement or excessive self-love dominates a person's personality and begins to have a negative impact on relationships, narcissism becomes increasingly troublesome.

Narcissistic Personality Disorder is the most severe end of the spectrum, where the person may appear grandiose or more covert in their demand for excessive attention and adulation.

These behaviors can include boasting, talking about oneself, needing to dominate conversations, or having one's needs or opinions take precedence over those of others. or they may seek reinforcement and attention through highly visible acts of service, self-sacrifice, or they may appear highly vulnerable and require others to continually cater to them and meet their needs. It can be very challenging to be in a relationship with someone who lacks empathy or respect for the needs or rights of others. This can result in verbal, emotional, and even physical abuse in some situations.

One source of anguish in a relationship with a narcissist is what is known as gas-lighting, which occurs when truth or reality is distorted, causing the other person to feel confused, undermined, and even begin to doubt their own vision of reality and memory. In a relationship with a narcissistic person, the other person's self-worth may be destroyed, which can lead to patterns of co-dependence over time as the individual modifies their behavior to primarily suit the wants of the narcissistic person.

Trauma frequently leads to the development of intense narcissistic tendencies. Some people with a high narcissism score can gain insight into their behavior and possibly improve if they are prepared to engage in therapeutic work. Unfortunately, it is typically work colleagues, partners, and adult children of very narcissistic persons who present to treatment with a legacy of grief and misery from their experiences.

Narcissistic partnerships are notoriously difficult. Narcissistic spouses typically struggle to fully love someone else because they do not truly love themselves. They are so preoccupied with themselves that they are unable to "see" their partner as a separate individual. They only see the partner in terms of how they meet (or fail to meet) their needs.

Their friends and children are only valued if they can supply these requirements. Narcissistic partners frequently lack empathy for their partners' feelings. This lack of empathy causes a great deal of pain.

Nonetheless, many people are attracted to narcissistic relationships. Narcissistic spouses can be quite enticing, especially at first.They are popularly known for having a "big" personality.

They are the life and soul of the party. They can make you believe that you must be exceptional in order for them to choose you. However, they can become too controlling in relationships over time. They could be envious or easily hurt. Narcissistic injuries frequently lash out and can be cut. Their reactions are intense and need attention.

"The effects of narcissism are most significant in relation to interpersonal functioning," says narcissistic personality expert Dr. W. Keith Campbell. In general, characteristic narcissism is connected with acting in such a way that one is seen as more likable in first meetings with strangers—but this likability fades with time and increasing exposure to the narcissistic individual."

This is why many people who have been in long-term narcissistic relationships describe an extremely passionate and thrilling honeymoon time at first, followed by a precipitous downturn as likability declines and self-centered behaviors rise. Narcissists are prone to falling madly in love with someone and committing quickly. This first passion and dedication, however, is difficult to maintain.

You may feel really lonely if you are in a narcissistic relationship. You may believe that you are nothing more than a prop, and that your wants and needs are meaningless.

Narcissistic partners act as if they are always correct, that they know better, and that their spouse is incompetent or wrong. This frequently results in the other person in the relationship becoming upset and attempting to protect themselves, or associating with this poor self-image and feeling horrible about themselves.

6.4 STRATEGIES FOR DEALING WITH A NARCISSISTIC PARTNER

If you find yourself in a narcissistic relationship, you can first recognise what you've done and consider the underlying factors that drove you to choose such a partner.

Did you have a selfish parent? Are you more at ease with your partner being in charge, allowing you to be more passive?

Do you feel more valuable because you are associated with someone who is in the spotlight?

Is the negative image of yourself that they create through their criticisms and superior attitudes compatible with your own critical ideas about yourself?

Many people who fall in love with narcissists struggle with codependency. They will tolerate some abuse because they lack confidence in themselves to set limits or stand on their own.

It is critical to understand your function in the narcissistic relationship. You can then begin to push yourself to change your portion of the equation. This, in turn, will challenge your spouse to alter their communication approach.

You can recognise your partner's low self-esteem and show compassion for the reality that his or her inflated sense of self, superiority, and grandiosity is a mask for self-hatred and feelings of inadequacy. You can also boost your self-esteem and self-worth by practicing self-compassion.

Don't let yourself be a victim. Act and respect your partner like an equal in all interactions.

CHAPTER 7

7.1 NARCISSISTIC ABUSE

Narcissistic abuse is a sort of emotional abuse that can profoundly modify a person's beliefs, feelings, and actions. It is also known as narcissistic abuse syndrome or narcissistic victim syndrome.

While narcissistic features are frequent in humans, it's important to note that narcissism can be a symptom of a bigger personality problem known as narcissistic personality disorder. Individuals suffering with this illness have an exaggerated sense of self-importance and desire attention and appreciation from others.

However, beneath their confident exterior, they frequently suffer from thoughts of inadequacy and are easily affected by criticism. A spouse with narcissistic traits may appear pleasant and kind at first, but their behavior can become manipulative, domineering, and exploitative with time.

What Signs Indicate Narcissistic Abuse?

It may be easier to identify narcissist abuse syndrome signs in someone other than oneself. Narcissistic spouses are skilled at controlling your thoughts, emotions, and behavior. Even children's mental health suffers when their parents are narcissistic. Some of the following indicators of narcissistic abuse can be revealed by insight and assistance from loved ones.

•You are lonely and estranged from your friends and family.

•You have a negative attitude towards everyone.

•You have difficulty making decisions at home, work, and for your family.

•You are unable to confront or leave your narcissistic partner.

•You're always worried that you've done something wrong.

•You lose your sense of self and identify with your violent narcissistic partner.

•You experience anxiety or depression symptoms, as well as unexplained physical issues.

•Physical symptoms can include changes in appetite, difficulty sleeping, exhaustion, and gastrointestinal issues. Manipulation and abuse are frequently so subtle that observers fail to recognise it as abuse.

You may be perplexed or even guilty, but you do not fully comprehend what is going on. Friends and relatives may not always believe a victim of narcissistic abuse, and you may doubt yourself. They may even challenge your interpretation of events and convince you that you misunderstood, which feeds the narcissist's attempts.

How to Spot the Symptoms of Narcissistic Abuse

•Long-term abuse and degrading behavior: can lead to a person believing they deserve to be emotionally abused. It's common to feel depleted in a relationship with a narcissist - cognitively, physically, and emotionally.

They may be unaware of the hurt they are creating since they are only concerned with achieving their immediate goal.When this happens,the abusive behavior may fade off,but will re-emerge when they long for something new. These are some symptoms of narcissistic abuse.

•Controlling Behavior : As the narcissist demands more time and attention, his or her behavior worsens. For a narcissist, control is synonymous with power.

•Isolation on a social level:
Narcissistic abusers isolate their spouses, reducing the victim's support system and making the abuse easier to continue. The narcissist becomes the only person who can provide validation, support, and affection.

•Mistrust:
As the victim's social isolation worsens, he or she may begin to distrust others. This is

exacerbated by the narcissist's lies and manipulation, which causes the victim to rely completely on their abuser for the "truth."

•Abuse of language:
Insults, put-downs, and verbal jabs aimed at demeaning the victim.

•Ignoring Borders:
Abuse victims are not permitted to make their own decisions or to be physically separated from their abuser. Invasion of digital privacy is included.

It is possible to recover from Narcissist abuse only if you're willing to learn more about the most effective trauma and abuse therapy.

Censorship:
Victims experience hypervigilance and racing thoughts, as if they are walking on eggshells. Victims always anticipate how an abusive partner will respond in order to please the abuser.

Excuses for inappropriate behavior:
Victims justify or cover up the abusers' harmful behavior. They may believe the excuse or it may be a form of self-preservation.

7.2 EFFECTS OF NARCISSISTIC ABUSE ON THE BODY AND MIND

A toxic relationship with a narcissist can cause mind and physical trauma, such as low self-esteem, panic attacks, and mental diseases such as anxiety and depression. A narcissistic parent's actions are deemed child abuse. Here are five other ways narcissistic abuse affects your mind and body.

When you respond to narcissistic abuse, what happens?

The clinical diagnosis of narcissistic personality disorder is characterized by a need for adulation and a lack of empathy for others. Individuals with narcissistic personality disorder may become upset when confronted or held responsible for their conduct, which is tied to a narcissistic injury that occurred to the individual earlier in their life.

Because narcissists appear entitled on the outside, it might be difficult to perceive that they harbor guilt and low self-esteem. When challenged with their behavior, the natural tendency is to blame others, deny they did anything wrong, or become upset.

Domestic violence and physical abuse can result from this. When confronted, a narcissist is unable to reflect on their actions or mistakes because doing so brings them to a knowledge of their trauma or narcissistic injury. The natural reaction is to blame the person and refuse to admit that anything is wrong with them.

Narcissists are judgmental for the same reason. What they perceive in themselves, they see in others. While they are unable to own their own errors, they may point out what is wrong with others, giving them a sense of superiority.

What symptoms do people exhibit when they are emotionally abused by a Narcissist?

•When a victim is caught up in a narcissistic abuse cycle, it can be difficult to define or label the experience since narcissists are adept manipulators who can warp reality to fit their desires.

•Victims may experience dissociation, a state in which they feel emotionally or physically disconnected from their surroundings. This interferes with their perspective of reality and memory.

•Victims may neglect their own needs in order to please a narcissistic abuser. Chronic stress caused by emotional and psychological abuse can lead to physical health problems such as premature aging, weight gain or loss, and immune system suppression.

•Victims of narcissistic abuse syndrome may experience self-harming tendencies or suicidal ideation in addition to the despair and anxiety that are linked with the syndrome.

•Chronic exhaustion
•Long-term stress
•Loss of self-esteem
•Damage to the brain
•Self-harming behavior

This is one of the most typical effects of narcissistic abuse on your health. Consider the abuser to be an energy vampire who drains your vital force.

Victims of narcissistic abuse have difficulty sleeping and lack ambition and energy to do anything.

Symptoms and signs of narcissistic abuse syndrome

Because the long-term impacts of narcissistic victims syndrome can lead to potentially life-threatening abusive behavior, narcissistic abuse syndrome can be lethal. Depression and anxiety can raise the risk of suicide or substance abuse disorder.

Long-term abuse can alter the brain of a victim, resulting in cognitive deterioration and memory loss. Changes in the brain, in turn, can raise the risk of chronic stress, PTSD, and self-sabotage symptoms. Individuals in rehabilitation from a narcissistic relationship experience emotions of perplexity, procrastination, low self-esteem, fear of failure, and worthlessness.

A narcissistic abuser may utilize financial exploitation to keep the victim in the relationship. They can restrict financial access, seize control of the victim's income, or engage in narcissistic manipulation and harassment.

7.3 RELATIONSHIPS OF NARCISSISTIC WOMEN

In relationships, narcissists women are developmentally stunted and cannot completely reciprocate emotional and sexual affection. Female Narcissists struggle to see partners' points of view, consider their needs, and make concessions. Narcissists have intense feelings such as jealousy, embarrassment, or narcissistic anger.

Narcissists frequently criticize spouses for failing to meet expectations or accuse them of not being loving, supportive, or appreciative enough. Because of their incessant demand for attention, often known as narcissistic supply, narcissist relationship patterns are also draining.

When Should You Leave a Narcissistic Partner?

Narcissistic partners frequently engage in narcissistic abuse, employing abusive strategies to conceal their negative characteristics and control their relationships. This can sometimes lead to narcissistic abuse syndrome in couples.

Emotional, physical, or sexual abuse, as well as sexual coercion, should never be allowed and should always be reasons for quitting a relationship.

Here are some reasons to end a relationship with a narcissist:

•You are physically abused.
•You are being abused or coerced sexually.
•Your lover is continuously keeping an eye on you.
•You are being emotionally duped.
•You are the victim of narcissistic gaslighting.
•You are being made fun of, intimidated, or dismissed.
•You have continuous anxiety or despair as a result of your relationship.
•Your partner is overly envious.

- You are estranged from friends and relatives.
- You're starting to use substances to cope.
- You are considering self-harm.

COPING STRATEGIES

Living with someone who exhibits narcissistic characteristics has distinct obstacles. So we turned to a best-selling book and narcissism specialist for advice.

We all have some healthy assertiveness and a desire to prioritize our own needs from time to time. This type of self-advocacy allows us to maintain our confidence and appreciate our achievements.

It's a different story with narcissism. Living with someone who exhibits narcissistic behaviors can be a distressing experience for many people.

If you have a housemate or loved one like this, realize that you are not alone and that help is available.

There are numerous strategies to assert your authority and cope.

Do you live with someone who exhibits narcissistic tendencies?

When interacting with someone who exhibits narcissistic characteristics, you may feel befuddled, frustrated, or invalidated. You may also be wondering why they act this way.

That is understandable. People that exhibit narcissistic behaviors may be unaware of how their activities have harmed you, either due to neurological abnormalities (as some study has found) or a lower ability to empathize with others.

According to 2018 research, narcissistic behavior may be the result of childhood trauma and neglect.

Viewing their habits from this perspective can be beneficial: They may be someone who desires affection, acceptance, and validation but doesn't know how to acquire it in a genuine way.

Quick Strategies For Coping With A Narcissist

•Define non-negotiable boundaries.
•Recognise the symptoms of gaslighting.

•Remove yourself from emotional outbursts.

•Learn the art of bargaining.

•Improve your self-esteem and self-soothing abilities.

•Create a close and knowledgeable inner circle.

Whether your flatmate or loved one has been diagnosed with NPD or you suspect that their behavior fits the criteria, there are numerous approaches you can take to deal with their narcissistic tendencies.

1. Define non-negotiable boundaries:
"Boundaries are very much an inside job," says Dr. Ramani Durvasula, a clinical psychologist in Los Angeles and author of two books on narcissism. "Setting boundaries doesn't connote that you expect the other person's Behavior to change,but

rather marking boundaries in your mind of what's acceptable to you , tolerable and behaves in line with that, " she said.

For example ,if your boundaries are set on Communication or late coming and the boundaries are violated,then the choice is yours on what to do — but don't link that to their behavior." Say " I will not accept being spoken to that way" if they insist, then exit the space safely" when communication boundaries have been broken.

2. **Learn how to spot gaslighting:**
Gaslighting is a type of deception. It happens when someone employs deception to make you doubt yourself or your sanity. As a result, you may feel befuddled or uneasy, or you may lose confidence.

When someone gaslights you, you may hear:
"I was just joking."
"I never said that."
"That didn't happen."
"You're overreacting."
"I don't know what you're talking about."

To combat this, you should try to get as many exchanges in writing as possible. In your phone or diary, you can keep a record of crucial notes, dates, receipts, and quotes.

3. Remove yourself from emotional outbursts:

Engaging with someone during an emotional outburst is futile, according to Durvasula.Kindly "Disengage,as difficult as it is,do not take personally their outbursts, most especially if they are directed at you. Recognise that dysregulated behavior is not appropriate, especially if it is hurtful or damaging, and give yourself permission not to engage," she says.

According to Durvasula, you might indicate your inability to continue the conversation unless they approach you gently and healthily.
"You are not a punching bag in terms of psychology. You are not their therapist, and it is their obligation to learn to regulate. "It's not your responsibility to teach them," she says.

4. Learn the art of bargaining:
Because their empathy is restricted, people with narcissism may not respond to traditional communication or "I" statements. You may instead try to use the

same transactional or cause-and-effect language as they do, but to enforce your limits in a healthy way.

This is how it sounds: Instead of saying " I feel hurt each time you come late for date night " say this: "Our reservation is for 6pm" If you're not there by 6:15, I'm going to the movies with a friend. You are invited to join us, but I will not wait for you." Was this useful?

5. **Increase your self-esteem and self-soothing abilities:**

Durvasula emphasizes that it is a fallacy that only persons with poor self-esteem wind themselves in these dynamics. "Many people with a strong sense of self get stuck in these relationships for a bunch of reasons, " she said. You can self-soothe by engaging in activities that make you feel good and increase your self-confidence, particularly activities that keep you from getting alone.

She adds that having a strong sense of self and being comfortable in your own company might help you set stronger limits.

6. **Create a close and knowledgeable inner circle:**

Durvasula recommends that you maintain a strong support network of people who are aware of this person's behavior, including finding a therapist who "gets" narcissism. A therapist can assist you in the following ways:

•Comprehend what is being placed.

•Resolving co-occurring issues.

•Assist you in developing a safety plan.

•Providing a safe environment for problem-solving.

•Confirm your experience.

•When to depart.

According to researchTrusted Source, persons who live with narcissism may be slow to adapt. You don't have to wait until the relationship becomes toxic, hazardous, or abusive before leaving. Durvasula suggests considering your next steps if you:
•Feel estranged from family and friends
•Mistrust your perception of reality
•Restate your arguments
•Justify their actions
•Repeatedly fall for deceptive promises

"If these things are happening, this relationship may no longer be healthy," she said.

Suggestions for healing after living with a narcissist.

It could take some time for you to recuperate. This process could take months for some. Years for others. Every individual is unique.
Consider the following to help you in your healing journey:
•Learning more about narcissism
•Developing new friendships
•Using your support network
•Journaling as a means of self-discovery
•Putting a stop to romantic relationships
•Collaborating with a therapist
"The end of a relationship with a narcissist is not an end," Durvasula explains.

She goes on to say that "it's actually a beginning and a real opportunity to take what happened as a lesson and a wake-up call to honor your authentic self, celebrate the opportunity that the end of this relationship brings, and view healing and growth as a lifetime process."

7.4 FIVE WAYS TO END A RELATIONSHIP WITH A FEMALE NARCISSIST

Breaking up with a narcissist can be difficult or easy depending on their state at the time of the split. If they are depleted or struggling to maintain their perfectionism, you will most likely encounter either overt or passive-aggressive wrath. On the other hand, they may suddenly become effusive and "love bomb" you in order to reclaim your affection. It might also be more challenging to decide how to end a relationship with someone you live with. It's best to be prepared for anything.

Here are five ways to end a relationship with a narcissist:

1. Make a List of Your Reasons for Ending the Relationship:

Give yourself examples from the past. People with personality disorders have dysfunctional ways of interacting with the world and, as a result, their behavior can readily distort reality. Their behavior can cause you to question your reality over time. You may be ready to leave, yet you may decide to stay because of their guilt or pleas.

Writing out your reasons for leaving the relationship and providing instances to yourself might help you re-ground yourself in reality during the separation process. Showing this list to the narcissist is unlikely to assist, so keep it for yourself rather than as "evidence" to persuade them of their wrongdoing.

2. **Make a Strategy:**

Consider your next steps after announcing the split and how the narcissist will react. If you live with a narcissist, for example, decide if you want to stay or urge them to leave. Have you made plans to go anywhere? Creating a plan will assist you during the potential counter-attack phase, when you may be moving rapidly and not thinking properly.

3. **Surround Yourself with Loyal People:**

Narcissists frequently isolate you from your support network. They expect intense loyalty or commitment, and you may have distanced yourself from friends or family during the relationship. Reconnect with those who truly have your back and inform them that you require assistance to quit this unhealthy relationship. You could even ask them to check in on you every day for the first few weeks as you adjust.

4. Get Rid of Any Reminders of the Relationship:

A narcissist may make you feel special by taking you on extravagant trips, giving you presents, or building a "magnificent" life with you. This might make remembering the sorrow of the dark times difficult while you work through the breakup.

Remove photos from your home and phone, and save or throw away any gifts that remind you of your relationship. If you want to save them, put them in a box, but be careful not to fall into the trap of thinking that things "weren't as bad" as you felt before the breakup.

5. Seek the Help of a Therapist:

A therapist can assist you in identifying concerns in a helpful manner that avoids denial. You may have "doubled down" on denial when living with a narcissist to avoid the pain of being criticized, neglected, exploited, or otherwise abused.

After a breakup, speaking with a trustworthy mental health expert to undergo therapy can help you rebuild your world. Your therapist can also assist you in exploring how your past may have made you prone to falling for a narcissist, so that you can avoid falling for one in the future. Finding the appropriate therapist might be time-consuming, but it is well worth the effort.

CHAPTER 8

8.1 QUITTING A NARCISSISTIC RELATIONSHIP

What to Expect When Breaking Up With a Narcissist:(5 Tips)

Because of their obsessive desire for adulation, harsh judgment, lack of empathy, and profound insecurities, it can be difficult to maintain a relationship with a narcissist.

If your partner is unwilling to work on their narcissistic qualities, the best thing you can do for your mental health is to leave. While breaking up with a narcissist is not easy, it is feasible if you have a good plan, understand their usual fury reactions, and seek expert support.

__What to Expect When breaking up /Divorcing a Narcissist__

Reactions to a breakup might vary depending on the type of narcissist and their state at the time of the breakup.

Remember that you are not in a relationship with a fully evolved person with an authentic self in any case, and they will react with defense mechanisms to avoid significant emotional pain and shame.

•A Simpler Breakup

If you are in a relationship with a grandiose narcissist who was never truly invested in you, the breakup may be easier. They'll gladly let you go and go on to the next dazzling object. They will, however, want to ensure that the "breakup story" makes them appear to be the ones who initiated the split. Taking this easy out may be a smart option if it is available.

•A More Difficult Breakup

Because narcissism is rooted in tremendous insecurity,narcissists will typically go on the attack if they cannot find a way to save face after receiving an injury.As a result, they may end up venting all of their rage onto you if they feel offended—this can be especially upsetting for empaths with narcissists. If this occurs, the best thing you can do is avoid engaging them and maintain firm limits.

A covert narcissist will be enraged if they feel devalued, will appear powerless, and will say they "gave you everything." They will portray you as a hateful, abandoning, heartless, and selfish person who has not appreciated what they've done in the relationship. When they feel abandoned, they may self-harm, threaten suicide, quit their job, or do other things to undermine themselves.

Last Thoughts

Narcissistic partners are often unable to accept responsibility for their actions. Consider what you can learn from the circumstance as you conclude a relationship that has lasted months or years.

Unfortunately, many mental health practitioners feel the prevalence of narcissistic personality disorders is rising.

However, learning to recognise a narcissist as a result of this experience will help you avoid future relationships with this sort of person.

Once you have healed from this breakup, you will be in a better position to locate a healthier partner and enjoy a more reciprocal, supportive relationship.

8.2 MOVING FORWARD AND HEALING

She just grew increasingly cruel to me, to the point that I feared there was something horribly wrong with me. I began seeing a therapist because I wondered, "What is wrong with me?" 'I am nothing.' She found something wrong with me every day. She'd tell me how awful I was, just awful stuff.

Mr Mark, a narcissistic abuse victim:
Victims of narcissistic abuse are trained to blame themselves, separate themselves from others, and believe they deserve severe treatment.

Women unlike men are better able to see through the abuser's manipulations and begin their path to safety when they understand more about narcissistic abuse and how to achieve safety.

Mr Mark's heartbreaking experience of being abused by a narcissistic abuser urges men to learn more about abuse and trauma and to seek help. Victims of Narcissistic Abusers Feel Inadequate.

For so many years, I blamed myself, believing that I needed to be better and that I wasn't good enough, and I was constantly striving to meet that ideal.

Mr Mark, a narcissistic abuse victim:
The subtle use of manipulation to make victims feel inadequate in every aspect is a powerful tool in every narcissistic abuser's toolbox.

Many victims believe they are: Because of the abuser's manipulations, many victims believe they are:

•Mothers who are terrible
•Mean
•Stupid
•Unwanted
•Useless
•Ugly
•Laz
•Crazy

Understanding that these very harmful views about oneself are universal among victims of narcissistic abuse may assist victims in understanding that they are not what their partner says or implies they are — in fact, they are frequently the polar opposite. Victims of Narcissistic Abuse are Tired

Victims are drawn into a reality where the abusive partner is at the center, and their life becomes about appeasing him because of the self-centered nature of abusers with narcissistic tendencies.

Narcissistic abusers frequently play the victim/martyr to guarantee that victims are so preoccupied with the abuser's feelings and "needs" that they don't have time or energy to practice self-care or recognise the abuse.

I was stuck in a cycle of trying to make her happy by giving her more and more and taking less and less and less from her. Mr Mark, a narcissistic abuse victim said:

One technique to determine if you are a victim of a narcissistic abuser is to ask yourself the following qualifying questions:

•Is it common for me to be drained and fatigued?

•Do I have trouble sleeping or sleep disturbances?

•Is my lover waking me up to chat, yell, or have sex with me?

•Do I spend a lot of time calming down my spouse, mending things that she is worried about, and working through relationship issues with her that seem to go in circles?

•Do I feel like I don't have time or energy to care for myself?

You may be a victim of narcissistic abuse if you responded yes to any of these questions.
Abusers who are narcissistic are master manipulators. I have earned two master's degrees. I should be able to see it, but you don't. You're not aware of it since they're skilled manipulators. I was perfectly fine with him making the world fit his needs. I simply went along with it.

Tragically, victims frequently blame themselves for failing to recognise the abuse earlier in the relationship. All men must recognise that narcissistic abusers are great manipulators who know just how to exploit each victim. You are not foolish, weak, or codependent if you succumb to her manipulation. You are simply the victim of a devious abuser.

Victims of Narcissistic Abuse Can Learn to Be Kind to Themselves. When men are subjected to this insidious form of marital abuse, they frequently suffer profound trauma.

This can emerge in a variety of ways, including:

•Physically (disordered sleep, fatigue, eating problems)
•Emotionally (swinging moods, strong emotions, numbness)

•Spiritually (disappointment or lack of trust)

•Psychologically (depression, anxiety)

•Even getting out of bed each morning feels like a Herculean task for many victims:

Any amount of just remaining alive every day was enough to get by.

Mr Mark ,a narcissistic abuse victim once said,

Victims who practice self-compassion, patience, and self-care will find it much easier to achieve safety and recovery.

Allowing yourself to feel the terrible feelings linked with trauma will help you overcome the crippling consequences of your partner's violence over time.

Betrayal Trauma Recovery Assists Narcissistic Abuse Victims

At BTR, we understand the anguish that a narcissistic abuser may cause his victim. Victims of narcissistic abuse deserve a safe environment to process their pain, talk to people who understand how they feel, ask essential questions, and connect with other victims.

You can join the Betrayal Trauma Recovery Group within your vicinity. Questions and Answers

8.3 WHEN TO SEEK PROFESSIONAL ASSISTANCE

Dealing with a narcissist may be challenging and exhausting, even if you have a strategy in place to help deflect or avoid their manipulation tactics. Seeking psychological treatment is recommended if you are unable to cope with the consequences of their acts or are suffering with connected trauma.

Couples or family therapy is not recommended if you are currently working on healing a relationship with a partner or family member.

This is due to the fact that a narcissist may utilize facts shared in therapy against the other person. However, in these circumstances, a therapist with experience working with couples in which one or both partners has NPD may be effective. Individual support and therapy, rather than couples therapy, is still advised

8.4 TREATMENT METHODS FOR NARCISSISTIC ABUSE VICTIMS

•Emotional Focussed Treatment (Eft): This type of therapy looks into the connection between feelings and emotions, as well as how they relate to or impact decision making.

•Attachment-based Therapy: investigates attachments and what causes anxiety or avoidance reactions in people in relationships. This type of therapy can help people figure out what makes them afraid to leave or stop a terrible relationship.

•CBT (cognitive behavioral therapy): CBT is excellent for learning how thoughts affect behaviors and for exploring any negative or self-limiting thoughts that arise in relationships.

•**Online Counseling:** This type of treatment might be good for persons who have hectic schedules or who work and reside in places where there are few options for mental health care. Many people also prefer online or telehealth therapy over regular therapy.

•**Group Therapy:** People who have experienced relationship trauma may benefit from group therapy because they can learn from the support and advice of others who have been in their shoes.

•**Somatic Therapy:** investigates the relationship between past traumas and how they are stored and experienced in the body. This strategy is effective for healing after a traumatic event.

Last Thoughts

Narcissists frequently use manipulation tactics to achieve more power and control, or to get what they desire. Many people who have witnessed these behaviors have expressed confusion and fear; please understand that this is a typical reaction. Seeking affirmation and support following a manipulative relationship is critical to recovery.

CAN A WOMAN CONFRONT AND CONQUER HER OWN NARCISSISM?

A female narcissist might challenge and overcome her narcissism by recognising and detaching from her critical inner voice's self-soothing, self-aggrandizing, and self-attacking attitudes. The views she adopted very early in their lives. She must recognise and address her negative attitudes towards herself and others. Voice Therapy is one approach for accomplishing this.

A Narcissistic woman must also distinguish herself from undesirable tendencies inherited from her parents or early carers, which she continues to exhibit in her current existence. Superior attitudes or condescending behaviors are examples of these characteristics.

She also had to let go of the modifications she had made in response to the ways her own parents ignored her or were emotionally hungry towards her. These adaptations may have been survival techniques in the past, but she now manages to push others away while sabotaging personal lives and objectives. Narcissistic women must also break the cycle of being self-centered or withholding.

They must resist the want to constantly compare oneself to others and the desire to be the "best" or "perfect" all of the time. Another approach to treating narcissism in women is to encourage self-compassion rather than self-esteem.

Dr. Kristin Neff, a psychologist, has conducted considerable research on self-esteem versus self-compassion. The distinction between self-esteem and self-compassion is that self-esteem focuses on judging oneself in comparison to others and emphasizes the need to be unique. Self-compassion is about "treating oneself with kindness, recognising one's shared humanity, and being mindful when considering negative aspects of oneself."

According to Dr. Neff's research, self-esteem leads to increased degrees of narcissism, whereas self-compassion does not. Self-compassion really combats narcissism by including the concept of a shared humanity with all other human beings, which leads to increased compassion for others. Self-compassion also encourages true self-awareness, which many narcissists lack, by encouraging us to be observant of our flaws, which is the first step towards addressing undesirable tendencies in oneself.

To regain a decent relationship from a narcissistic relationship, the narcissist must overcome their self-centered and bad characteristics. They must confront their self-feeding habits and phony independence. They must concentrate on increasing their empathy and regard for others.

Finally, people must establish transcending aims, caring for and investing in the well-being of others. Being charitable and giving to others are examples of corrective behaviors, as are developing true self-esteem and practicing focusing outside of oneself.

FREQUENTLY ASKED QUESTIONS ABOUT NARCISSISTS.

1. How prevalent are female narcissists?

According to study, 4.8% of females and 7.7% of males have narcissistic personality disorder (NPD).

2. Is it possible for a narcissistic lady to change?

Continuous and strict counseling, as well as a commitment to improve, can help a narcissist transform. Counseling may not produce the expected effects if the individual is unwilling to change.

3. What are some of the possible reasons for female narcissism?

It is critical to recognise that the development of narcissism is a complex process impacted by a variety of circumstances. Parental overindulgence, excessive praise, or overvaluation, as well as inconsistent or inattentive parenting, can all lead to the development of narcissistic behavior.

The development of narcissistic tendencies can be influenced by societal and cultural influences. Childhood trauma, such as emotional, physical, or sexual abuse, can also result in the development of narcissistic characteristics.

4. What effect does a woman's narcissism have on her parenting style and connections with her children?

Individuals that are narcissistic frequently struggle to empathize with others, even their children. They may struggle to grasp their children's feelings and needs. She may prioritize her own need for attention and praise over serving the needs of her children. Narcissistic mothers frequently demonstrate inconsistent parenting techniques, which can cause children to become confused and anxious.

5. What are some of the most popular myths about narcissistic women?

There are some popular myths about narcissistic women that might lead to stereotypes and misunderstandings. One common misperception is that narcissistic women are always haughty. It is commonly considered that narcissistic women are constantly self-assured and confident.

6. How can society confront and prevent the detrimental effects of narcissism, especially in women?

To address and avoid the detrimental effects of narcissism, a multifaceted approach including individuals, groups, and society as a whole is required. Individuals who develop empathy and emotional intelligence skills are better able to understand and relate to the experiences and feelings of others. Encouragement of different social relationships and support networks can aid in the prevention of narcissistic tendencies.

Being in a relationship with a narcissistic partner can have a negative impact on your mental health and self-esteem. You end yourself blaming yourself for everything because narcissistic women blame you for their sins and acts.

However, when dealing with such a connection, it is critical not to lose sight of what is right and wrong. Your emotions are legitimate, as is your desire for a good partnership. As a result, set clear limits, speak up for yourself, and get assistance if you feel you can't handle it on your own.

SUMMARY AND CONCLUSIONS

The Book "She's Notorious: Unveiling Overt and Covert Narcissistic Traits in Females" discusses the emergence of narcissistic traits in women. It distinguishes between overt and covert narcissistic behaviors, offering light on how these traits may manifest differently in females than in males.

The author explores the influence of narcissistic traits on interpersonal interactions, highlighting the possibility of manipulation and a lack of empathy. According to the essay, recognising these characteristics is critical for understanding and navigating interactions with people who display narcissistic behavior.

Finally, the study emphasizes the need of knowledge and education in recognising narcissistic behaviors in females, creating healthier connections, and boosting emotional well-being in both personal and professional settings.